Warning!

Before you read this book, you should know that skating can be dangerous. If you are not careful, and even sometimes if you are, you can break bones, including that hard skull that wraps up your brain. This book explains skating, but it is not intended to be used as a training manual. If you plan to get up on skates, protect yourself by taking a few lessons, using the right equipment, always skating with a buddy, and only doing tricks that you're ready for.

A NOTE ABOUT HELMETS: When you participate in extreme skating events, protect your head! It's what you use to see, hear, eat, think, talk, and live. You don't want to break it!

Also, if you do go out and break your head, or any other part of your body or anyone else's body, don't blame National Geographic. We didn't tell you to do it. We told you to be careful!

(Translation into legalese: Neither the publisher nor the author shall be liable for any bodily harm that may be caused or sustained as a result of conducting any of the activities described in this book.)

One of the world's largest nonprofit scientific and educational organizations, the National Geographic Society was founded in 1888 "for the increase and diffusion of geographic knowledge." Fulfilling this mission, the Society educates and inspires millions every day through its magazines, books, television programs, videos, maps and atlases, research grants, the National Geographic Bee, teacher workshops, and innovative classroom materials. The Society is supported through membership dues, charitable gifts, and income from the sale of its educational products. This support is vital to National Geographic's mission to increase global understanding and promote conservation of our planet through exploration, research, and education.

For more information, please call 1-800-NGS LINE (647-5463) or write to the following address:
National Geographic Society
1145 17th Street N.W.
Washington, D.C. 20036-4688 U.S.A.
Visit the Society's Web site at www.nationalgeographic.com.

NATIONAL GEOGRAPHIC

EXTREME Sports

SKATE!

Your Guide to Inline, Aggressive Vert, Street, Roller Hockey, Speed Skating, Dance, Fitness Training, and More.

BY MICHAEL SHAFRAN

Illustrations by Jack Dickason

NATIONAL GEOGRAPHIC

WASHINGTON, D.C.

What's Inside

Glide to Glory

See what it's like to fly...
with both feet on the ground.

et ready to roll . . . and rock.

You've tried walking. You've tried running. Now see what it's like to roll, glide, and cruise—on your own two feet. On skates, you can go anywhere. Just keep your balance.

Skating offers many options for fun. You can work on going fast or practice cool moves like the crossover and the swizzle; you can go vertical, you can dance, you can race. And the great thing is, you don't need an ice rink or a lot of special gear. Just you, your skates, pads, and helmet, and any wide-open pavement.

If you love speed and want to build strength, you've picked the right sport. Want to catch some speed? Want to learn what it takes to master a radical move off the half-pipe? Want to know about the pros and get yourself sponsored? Get in line or make strides on your own. Skating is all about getting ahead.

With skates, you'll go far—and fast!

Extreme Sports

Part One

Fundamentals

- Getting Started
- Gearing Up
- The Pros Know
- Those Are the Brakes
- Now You're Road Ready

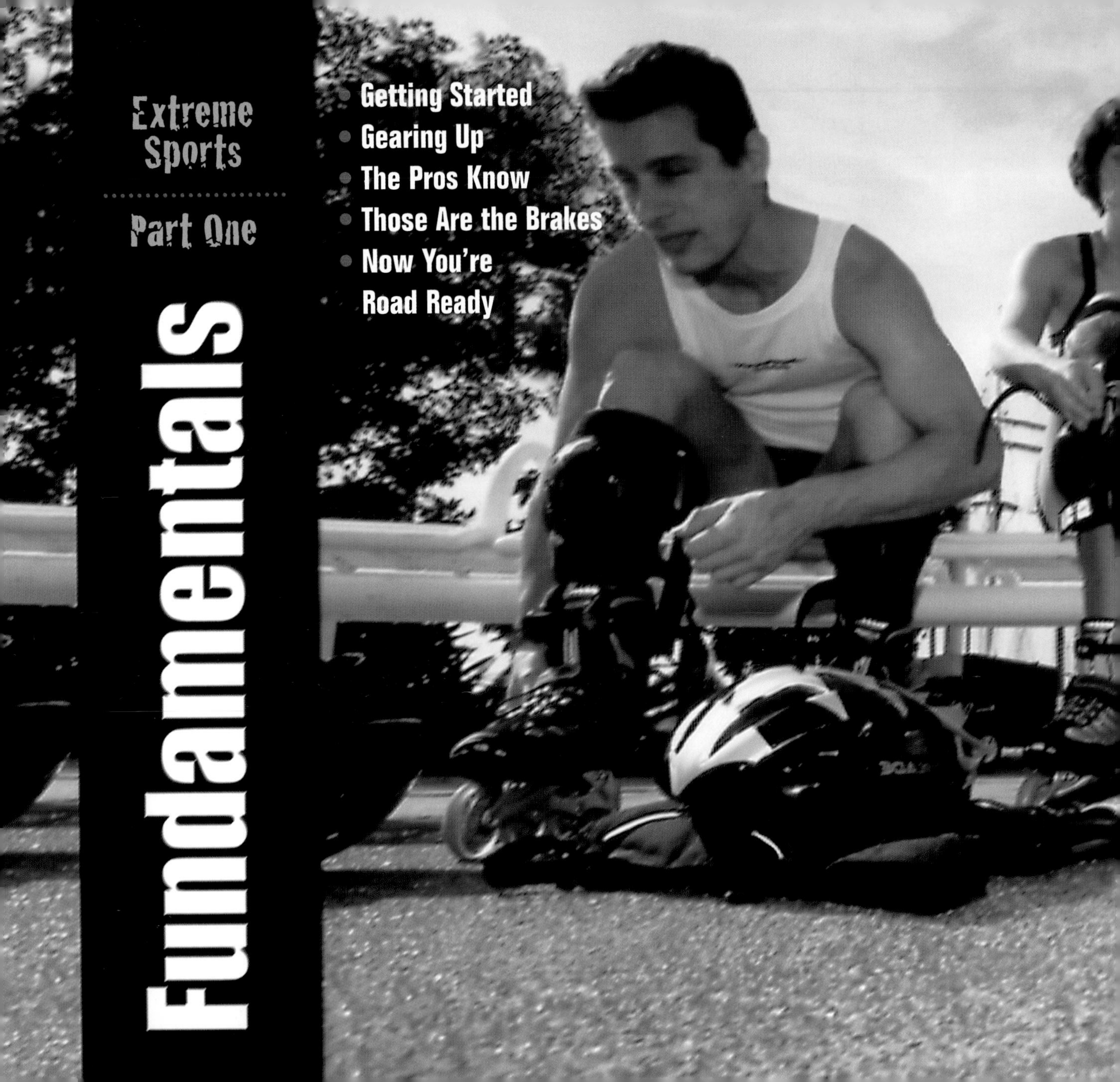

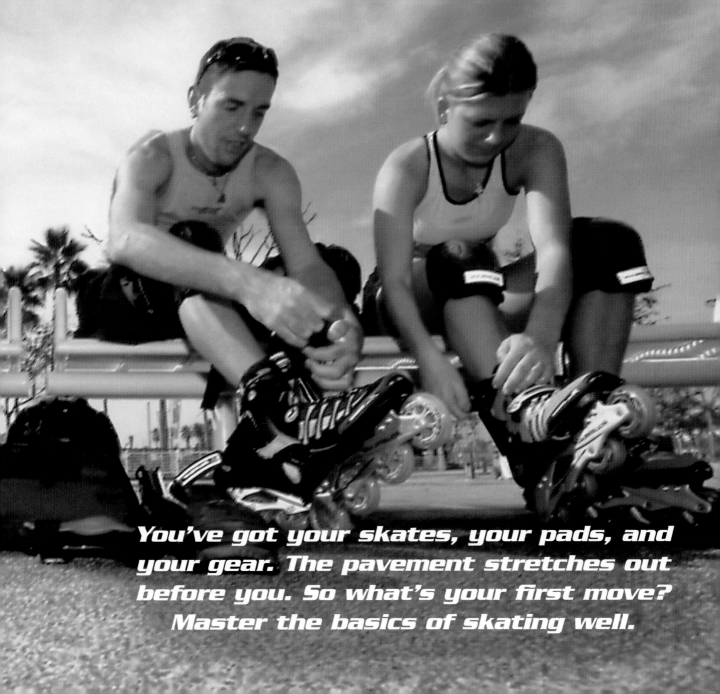

You've got your skates, your pads, and your gear. The pavement stretches out before you. So what's your first move? Master the basics of skating well.

Getting Started

In the world of skating, living is easy: no entry fees and no mind-boggling rules. Just strap on some simple gear and get moving. It's just you, four wheels on each foot, and the road ahead.

You'll never walk again—and who wants to, if you can skate? Every time you throw on a pair of skates, you step out of the pedestrian world and into a smoother, speedier dimension. So stretch out those legs, give a good push, and get rolling.

GET READY TO ROLL

You can start skating virtually anywhere. But the best starting place is flat and hazard-free. Carpets and grass are great places to stand in your skates for the first time because you won't roll away. Here, practice the "ready position," the standard, stable skating stance: Bend your knees until you can't see your toes; keep your feet shoulder-distance apart, your arms slightly bent, hands out and relaxed; and look straight ahead. You're now ready for takeoff.

GET ON EDGE

Look at your wheels. Each has left and right edges that, when angled, make the skate turn and help it grip the asphalt. Outside edges are the sides of the wheels that face away from your body. Inside edges are on your instep and face the opposite skate. Get to know your edges—they're crucial if you want to make all the right moves.

GO FOR A SPIN

Enough talking; it's time for action. Pick any place that's smooth and flat: an empty parking lot, a wood-floored room, or a roller-skating rink. Get in the ready position. Then form your skates into a V, with your heels in and toes out. Gently walk your right skate forward—stepping ahead rather than outward—and push with the left. Now walk your left skate forward and push with your right. As you continue to walk your skates, try to glide after each step. You're now officially a skater.

TRY FALLING (REALLY!)

Yes, it's the last thing you want to do. But when you fall—and you will fall—you should know what to do, so it's best to practice ahead of time. First, anytime you feel like you're about to bite it, put your hands on your knees. This prevents the panicked "reach for the sky" position: upstretched hands, which shift your weight up and back and—whammo!—you land on your butt or noggin. To practice falling, reach for your knees and lean forward until you fall onto your kneepads (you're wearing all the pads, right?) and then slide forward onto your wrist guards. As you go down, keep your fingertips up to distance them from the asphalt. See, it's not so bad. You've now had your first fall. Congrats!

Gearing Up

Skates have come a long way from the early days of metal wheels and leather straps. Check out the latest innovations in gear.

Unlike some other sports, skating doesn't require a lot of special gear. No poles, no boards, no goggles, or wetsuits. But it's important to know what you do need before you get started.

INLINE ANATOMY

Remove all the nuts, bolts, and rivets from a roller skate, and you're left with a boot. The boot is the outside layer of a skate. Plastic or hard, boots usually have padded linings and are more stable and durable. Soft boots are lighter and more flexible. The shaft that holds the wheels in place is called the frame. Plastic frames offer more value, while composite and pricier aluminum frames are faster. Axle bolts screw everything into place.

GET PROTECTION

It's a guarantee that if you skate, you will fall. A hard fall can happen even at a standstill. You'll get the most use out of wrist guards, which can turn a painful fall into an easy slide. More important, however, is a helmet, which will protect your head. Add a pair of knee and elbow pads, and you have all the necessary armor to battle the forces of gravity.

GET A ROUND

The wheels on a skate range widely in size (measured in millimeters) and hardness (ranked by a "durometer" A scale). The higher the A scale number, the harder the wheel. Recreational skates have wheels with a hardness of 77A to 80A. Smaller wheels are lower to the ground and more stable, while larger wheels go faster. Softer wheels offer more grip and shock-absorption, whereas harder wheels are speedy and longer-lasting.

GET YOUR BEARINGS

Bearings make your wheels spin, so keep them away from evil substances like dirt, water, and hair. Bearings are rated on a scale called the ABEC standard, which ranges from 1 to 7. Generally, the higher the number, the faster the bearing. But don't just shop by the numbers—many popular Swiss bearings aren't even rated. Instead, get advice from a knowledgeable skater or shop techie.

TECH TALK

Know your skate's inner parts—look at the diagram on page 61 for more detailed information.

BEARINGS: Cylinders inside each wheel that contain tiny steel balls.

CAGE: Piece that holds the balls in a bearing.

HUB: The hard plastic center of a wheel.

RIVET: A machine-inserted metal piece that holds buckles and other skate parts to the boot.

SPACER: The plastic or metal piece that keeps apart the two bearings inside a wheel.

SPEED LACES: Systems that let you lace up with a single tug.

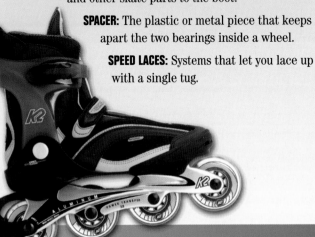

The Pros Know

The best way to learn skating is from a pro. Let someone show you how it's done, and then don't forget to practice.

Once you've got the basics down, you're ready for the real deal. To learn quickly and properly, take a series of lessons with a certified International Inline Skating Association (IISA) instructor. In the meantime, here are some solid moves to practice on your own.

STRIDE

To move faster and with greater ease, you need to push, or "stride," properly. The correct form is to stride straight out to the side, not push backward. Skating is all about resistance, and you get the most by pushing off your heel directly to your right or left.

SWIZZLE

It's time to get those feet apart. Put your feet in the V position and push both skates out until they're past shoulder-width apart. Next, using your inner thigh muscles, pull your legs together again until the skates nearly touch. Push back out and repeat. The swizzle is great for skating backward and perfecting slalom crisscrosses (see pp. 52–53).

TURN

To go in a new direction, point your head to the far left or right, and your feet will miraculously follow. If you want more decisive turns, shift your weight onto the side you're turning toward. If you're going right, for example, this will get your wheels onto their right edges. Then put pressure on the skate on the opposite side of where you're going.

DUCK THE HAZARDS

Obstacles are everywhere: cracks, bumps, drops, debris. Always roll around the big hazards. If there's something smaller, ride roughshod. Staggering is the key for manhole covers, small twigs, and uneven surfaces. To stagger, roll one skate forward and drop the other behind, placing all your weight onto your heels. This makes you more stable by spreading out your wheelbase. Staggering is also essential for skating off curbs, landing from jumps, riding stairs, and mastering the half-pipe.

LEARN THE LINGO

BLACK ICE: Perfectly smooth asphalt, sometimes mixed with shiny glass particles.

BLOWOUT: Occurs when a wheel loses a chunk of its tire or separates from the hub.

BONK: Occurs when you run out of energy mid-skate. (Be sure to eat a light meal before skating and snack during long skates.)

FACE PLANT: Occurs when your nose beats your hands to the pavement. Ouch!

GATORBACK: A road so rough it makes your toes go numb.

RASPBERRY: The colorful scrape you get from putting skin to asphalt, a.k.a. "road rash."

ROCKER: A skate with the middle two wheels lowered for tighter and easier turns.

A skater hits a hazard. ▼

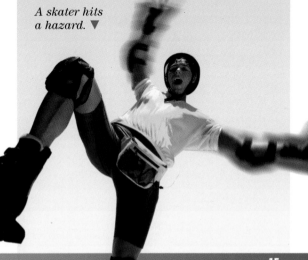

Those Are the Brakes

There are many different ways to stop on skates. Find out what feels right, what suits your style, and what works best in any number of skating situations you'll encounter.

Learning to stop is the one true way of becoming a free spirit on skates. Once you've mastered the standard heel brake, hills lose much of their menace and traffic crossings become a cinch. So rather than tumbling onto the grass or desperately lunging for lampposts, become a star braker. Here's how.

HEEL BRAKING 101

There are fancier ways to stop, but none work better than the standard heel brake. It's relatively quick, it doesn't kill your wheels, and it's easy to learn. All you have to do is break it up into four simple steps:

❶ **START IN THE READY POSITION:** Have your knees bent, hands out, and eyes forward.

❷ **STAGGER:** Roll the braking skate forward so that its heel is past the toe of the non-braking skate. If you have trouble rolling the front foot out straight, squeeze your thighs together.

❸ **TOE LIFT:** Raise the toe of your braking skate until you feel the heel brake's rubber drag on the pavement.

❹ **SIT:** This is the key to actually stopping rather than just slowing down. Aim your hips (not your shoulders) at the ground and sink into a squat. Transfer 90 percent of your weight onto the brake, pushing it forward if you have to.

ALL THE STOPS

There are plenty of other ways to slam on the brakes, and each has its benefits and drawbacks. Remember that if you're not using the heel brake, you're eating into your wheels. But practice stopping different ways so that you'll be prepared to screech to a halt in virtually any situation.

Heel Brake

T-STOP: Also called the J-stop, which bears a closer resemblance to the actual move.

● Lunge forward onto one skate.
● Let the other skate drift behind you.
● The wheels of your rear skate will drag along the ground, slowing you down.
● To boost stopping power, pull in the rear skate.

The heel brake can interrupt a skater's momentum by hindering advanced moves. That's why the T-stop is best for rough and debris-covered surfaces and is a must for experienced speed, aggressive, hockey, dance, and slalom skaters.

BACKWARD: When skating backward, the heel brake is unusable. Instead, bend your knees deeply and lift up and extend the stopping skate behind you. Then lower the wheels to the ground. Make sure that they are tilted enough to slide, not grip.

POWERSLIDE: The ultimate in stylish stops. While speeding forward, spin around backward and lunge low. This thrusts out the wheels of your braking skate until they slide. It's like a backward stop, but you're still moving forward. Powerslides are best done fast and with a lot of attitude.

Now You're Road Ready

You've mastered the basics of stopping and rolling, but skating is more than just moving in a straight line. Learn about turning, climbing, and going backward.

Once you've got all of the core moves down, get ready for the big time. Put in the practice time and before you know it, the following moves will show everyone that you're a seasoned skater.

BACKSIDE BALANCE

Remember the swizzle? (see p. 15) Now try alternating swizzles one foot at a time, rolling out half-circles to gain momentum. Once you have that down, turn around and do the same thing in reverse. Just remember to stick out your backside for balance and to look over your shoulder.

HEADING FOR THE HILLS

Climbing is mostly about fitness, but a few techniques make it easier. First, swing your arms forward and back to help power your legs. Don't cross your hands past the center of your chest or you'll pull yourself off-balance. Also, instead of just putting the skate you push off from back down, roll it uphill for extra momentum.

REVERSING DIRECTION

Say you're going forward and you want to go back the way you came. Try this maneuver to reverse direction:

- Turn your body to one side.
- Place one foot in the opposite direction from where you're turning.
- Your back foot will angle outward, causing you to spin.
- When you've turned 180 degrees, flip your leading skate around.

Another option is to do a small jump and turn your hips and torso around while airborne. Keep your eyes looking ahead (they shouldn't turn with your body) and try to land firmly.

CUT CORNERS

This turn lets you speed up as you round a corner. Follow these steps for turning right:

1. Lean heavily to the left.
2. Push your left skate underneath you and outside to the right.
3. As you start to fall over, let your right skate come around.
4. Push out your right skate.
5. Catch yourself with your left skate.
6. Repeat.

If you're turning left, follow these steps but reverse left and right.

Tip: Forget about actually crossing over and concentrate on getting the pushing skate out of the way so the lifted skate can simply be placed down.

A skater does a crossover turn. ▶

Extreme
Sports

Part Two

Aggressive

- Vertical Horizons
- Hit the Streets
- Tricks for Kicks
- Competition Rules

Aggressive skating is where style and extreme sports meet, and it's not for the faint of heart. If you're looking to build your bag of tricks, this is the place: big airs, endless rails, jumping down stairs, grinding waxed curbs, and more. The X Games were partly built on the back of aggressive skating, and these days skate parks around the world are filled with fearless riders going for broke. Are you up to the challenge?

Vertical Horizons

When you go vertical, your wheels get light and you give yourself to the heavens above. Then you fall back down and start all over again.

Vert is the original competitive form of aggressive skating. Here, the daring take flight into and over the half-pipe, a large U-shaped ramp that can stand up to a whopping 12 feet high. Vert stands for vertical, and that's the direction you'll be going if you can make it all the way up the half-pipe walls: vertical up, then vertical down.

A skater executes a grab on both skates while airborne.

PIPE DREAMS

The bottom of a half-pipe's U shape is called the flat, and the rounded part where you begin to climb is the transition. High up the wall is the vert, the section that's completely perpendicular to the ground. The top of each wall is called the lip and is lined by a round metal pipe called the coping. This is where you do your grinds. At the top is the platform, where you wait your turn to drop in again.

UPS AND DOWNS

If you haven't ridden the half-pipe before, it's best to start at the bottom. Start by skating across the flat base, fast enough so that you begin climbing. Push your weight against the ramp floor in an exaggerated bounce and throw your arms upward to gain height. For better stability, stagger your feet on the transitions and keep your weight back as you climb. Once the momentum stops, you'll roll in reverse, so look backward. Pick up speed on the way down and roll with your feet together across the flat—don't skate unless you need more speed. Do the same in reverse as you head to the other side. Keep practicing until you can get higher and higher up the half-pipe walls.

DROPPING IN

Once you can skate up to a high point, you're ready to try dropping in from the top. To start, place your middle wheels over the coping. From here, commitment is the key. Bend deep and lean over your toes. As you dip, keep your weight forward. Feel the rush as gravity helps you glide down and then way up the other side. Mission control, we have liftoff.

RAMP IT UP

Master these vert moves, and you'll be on your way to the big time.

180-DEGREE TURNS: As you hit maximum height, turn your head and shoulders toward the ground and swerve around, facing forward. Try a small hop turn to get around faster.

STALLS: Once you get up by the coping, place your wheels onto the rail, let momentum swing you upright, and come to a stop. You've now stalled. Lean back or jump around to keep going.

GRABS: As you get air, reach down for one of your skates, grab it and pull it up, tweaking it as far up, out, or across as you can. The greater the contortion, the better.

FLIPS: Backward is easier than forward. As you get air, throw your feet over and then lift your head to finish up. Easy enough… *not!* ▶

INVERTS: As you approach the coping, reach down to grab the rail while your legs go airborne. It looks like a one-arm handstand. Pull an upside-down grab for added effect.

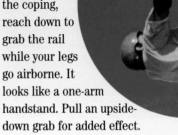

Hit the Streets

*The urban terrain is a street
skater's paradise: Skating innovators
transform ordinary concrete steps,
handrails, and curbs into a radical arena.*

Street skating comes from exactly where
you'd think: city playgrounds like
New York, Los Angeles, and other hot spots.
It all started with skaters making simple jumps
and curb grinds, getting chased off steps by security
guards, and riding just about anything, anywhere.
These days, street has evolved into a full-blooded
skate culture with a worldwide competitive scene.

DAILY GRIND

Grinding means sliding your skates across curbs, rails, and anything else on which you can roll. You're actually sliding sideways, on the frames of your skates, rather than rolling on the wheels. The key to most moves is to have extra space between your wheels so that you slide along the frame. You'll need the right gear: In the middle of the skate, use two hard wheels smaller than the front and back wheels, or get an aggressive skate that spreads the wheels wider in the middle. When grinding, spread your legs out in a wide stance and keep them there.

STAIR BASHING

There are few things more satisfying than flying down a flight of stairs…without falling. Believe it or not, going backward is easier (you won't fall very far), as is going faster. Pick a short set of shallow stairs to start with. The golden rule is to stagger your feet and keep them apart, making sure to look behind you. You can also try going forward, but make sure to remove your brake or else it will bounce off the steps and send you flying. Hold out your hands for balance. Then relax and enjoy the ride.

RAMPS 'N' RAILS

Rail riding is a great rush, but it helps to be able to jump high enough. If you need a ramp, put together a standard launch ramp made from plywood. It looks like a lying-down J and is small enough to keep in a garage or a storage room. Other types include a spine ramp, which is two ramps

sharing a single coping; and a box, which is a square-ish platform connecting launch ramps, rails, and steps. Jumping takes a ton of practice: Leap higher and higher while making sure to stagger your feet for a stable landing.

STREET WHEELS

Different wheel setups on an aggressive skate allow different moves. Get the arrangement that's right for you.

STANDARD FLAT: The typical skate setup with relatively large and soft wheels. It's great for jumps, stairs, and ramps because of the stability of the long, flat wheelbase, but it's lousy for grinding.

ALL-SMALL: Smaller and harder wheels give you a big enough gap to grind while maintaining stability.

FLAT-ROCKER: This setup preserves some speed while still maintaining stability and space to grind standard rails. Use small outer wheels and even smaller middle wheels that are rockered down, or lowered, so that all four wheels lie flat on the ground.

ANTI-ROCKER: This setup uses larger wheels on the outside and small extra-hard ones in the middle. While you lose some control and speed, you can grind just about anything.

Tricks for Kicks

Aggressive is about getting down to it when you're grinding into that rail. It's also about catching air.

Aggressive skaters are making up new moves all the time. They get together in a "session" and show each other what they can do. If you've ever seen a session, you'll notice that they make it look easy. In fact, they got to be this good the old-fashioned way: by practicing. Next time you're skating at a session of your own, take a crack at some of these advanced moves.

Arms braced for balance, a skater grinds his way down a handrail.

GRINDING WITH GRACE

SOUL: A grind using the undersole of the rear, or soul, skate's boot.

ACID GRIND: A grind in which your rear foot is on the railing or curb and your front foot points in the opposite direction (instead of perpendicular to the railing, as in a standard grind).

ALLEY-OOP SOUL: The same grind as Soul, except using the forward skate.

X GRIND: A grind with the legs crossed and feet on opposite sides of the rail.

SWITCH STANCE: Changing to the opposite direction in the middle of a grind.

ROCKET: Reaching for your skates as your legs extend fully out in front.

HITTING THE AIR

CAMEL: Tapping your skate wheels (at the toe or heel) onto the top of a ramp.

DISASTER: A grind in which you launch way up high and aim for a railing. Guess what happens if you don't land it?

METHOD AIR: When airborne, grabbing your left skate with your left hand, or your right skate with your right hand.

MUTE AIR: When airborne, reaching in front of (or behind) your legs and grabbing the opposite skate. ▶

BIO: A spin done while vertical or near-vertical on a ramp.

MISTY FLIP: A forward flip in which you spin 540 degrees sideways (that's one complete turn and half of another) and land backward. Guaranteed to leave 'em stunned.

BRAINLESS: Spinning 540 degrees in the air while simultaneously back flipping.

LIP TRICK: Any stunt done in the lip of the ramp, usually along the coping.

REWIND: A spin into the ramp immediately following a lip trick.

FARSIDE: Jumping over a rail to land a grind on the opposite (far) side.

Competition Rules

For those looking to take their aggressive moves to a higher level, it's time to hit the competitions. There's a lot to choose from, depending on where you are and what moves you want to show off.

The top pros set their sights on the major competitions like the X Games, ASA (Aggressive Skaters Association) Pro Tour, or the Gravity Games. If you're just starting out, you're better off entering a grassroots event like the ASA Amateur Circuit or Monsters of Roll. At any level, the action is surprisingly supportive with skaters cheering each other rather than sneering at rivals.

GO FOR THE GOLD!

Most competitive events are timed, with two preliminary runs that last about a minute each. Skaters are judged on style, difficulty, consistency, and creativity. There's also a newer trend of having less formal street competitions in urban locales, as well as trick-matching comps like IMYTA (I Match Your Trick Association), where skaters mimic each other's moves in elimination rounds.

SPONSOR ME

The real prize for the aspiring aggressive skater is getting sponsored. A sponsorship can get you all the gear and equipment you need, or it can give you the glamorous life as a salaried pro. First off, you need to be good, so practice, practice, practice. Then aim for placements in your regional comps. Also, you need to be seen. Get out there and make friends with aspiring photographers. Have them take cool photos and then mail them to skate-friendly magazines. Finally, armed with some wins and a magazine appearance or two, put together a packet of your accomplishments and mail them to the skate companies of your choice.

PRO: AIR EDWARDS

Chris Edwards, nicknamed the "Airman" for his towering vert takeoffs, is a pioneer of grinding and other techniques. Edwards's competitive days are mostly behind him, but he's still an inspiration to soon-to-be aggressive skaters everywhere.

PRO: THE MONSTER

Jaren "The Monster" Grob captured both the ASA Pro title and X Games gold in 2001. The Utah native first caught the public's eye as a skater in the Ringling Bros. and Barnum & Bailey Circus, which he followed up with 1999 rookie-of-the-year honors on the ASA Pro Tour.

PRO: FABULOUS FABIOLA

Brazil's Fabiola da Silva is the world's top woman pro skater and X Games champ. From 1996 to 2000, da Silva won four out of five X Games women's vert competitions. Her best achievement, however, was the establishment of the Fabiola Rule in 2000, opening the way for women to compete in pro men's comps. It occurred after the ASA eliminated the women's vert field. "I can't give up," she said at the time. "I believe that girls can do it (win in a unisex format) and I am going to keep skating and trying my hardest." Since then, she's made the men's top 10 several times. Her best finish against men so far was second at the Latin American X Games Qualifier in March 2002.

Fabiola da Silva

Extreme Sports

Part Three

Roller Hockey

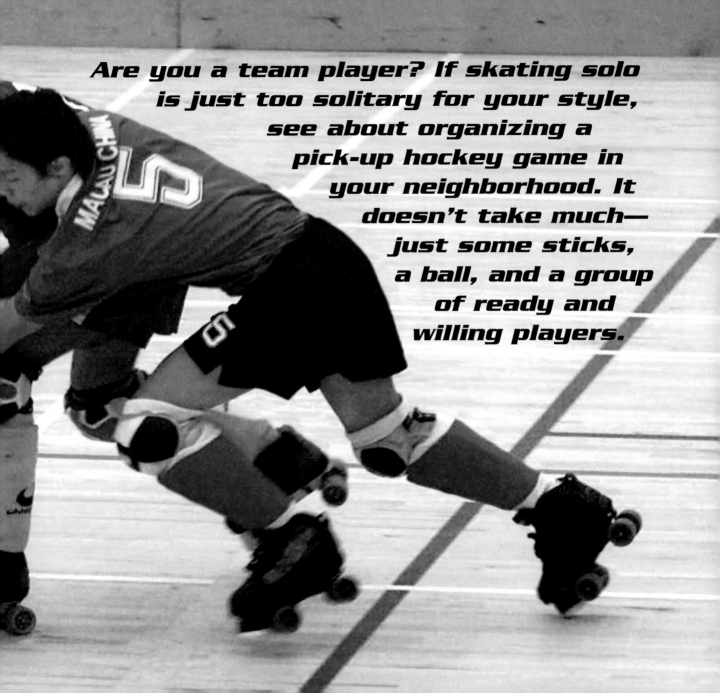

Are you a team player? If skating solo is just too solitary for your style, see about organizing a pick-up hockey game in your neighborhood. It doesn't take much— just some sticks, a ball, and a group of ready and willing players.

Goal-Oriented

Roller hockey is fast and exciting, and unlike its ice counterpart, roller hockey doesn't have bone-crunching body checks or play-stopping offside calls. Since official leagues usually feature just four players (plus goalies) per team, you get a super fast game with lots of opportunities to score.

While most types of skating are individually focused, roller hockey provides all of the action and spirit of the team game. And while you can happily buy tons of cool gear for the real deal, you can just as easily get going with a stick, pads, a ball, and a helmet. How officially you play is up to you.

PICK-UP STICKS

The easiest way to start is to buy a stick and a ball and head out to the local pick-up game—or start your own. All you need is an empty parking lot, a driveway, or any other open piece of pavement. Practice solo, play one-on-one, organize a five-on-five—it doesn't matter. You'll find that over time, you'll acquire better gear and someone might even show up with a proper net. The beauty of the pick-up game is its unorganized organization.

HEAD FOR COVER

For guaranteed year-round play and a structured game, nothing beats a proper indoor facility. Most offer league play, many with coaches. The surfaces vary from coated cement to wood to synthetic. What's best is a floor that's slippery enough for fast puck action and hockey stops, yet balanced with enough grip for strong skating. You'll usually have to shell out some cash for indoor access, but it's worth it when you find yourself with officiating, a lit scoreboard, and a proper penalty box for getting the goons out of your way.

HOCKEY SPEAK

ATTACKERS: Offensive players, who bring the puck into enemy territory.

BISCUIT: By any other name, a puck.

CREASE: The half-circle in front of the goal where offensive players can't score.

DASHERS: The boards that encircle the rink.

GRINDING: Not to be confused with its aggressive skate meaning, grinding in hockey occurs when two opposing players get crammed together fighting for the puck.

HAT TRICK: When a player scores three times in a game.

HIGH STICKING: Bringing the stick above your waist (not allowed).

HOOKING: When you wrap your stick around an opponent (also not allowed).

LINE: Teammates who play on the ice as a unit.

ONE TIMER: A pass that's hit into the goal.

POKE CHECK: Thrusting your stick at a puck in enemy hands in order to knock it to your teammate.

POWER PLAY: When one team has more players in the penalty box than the other, the team with more players on the ice has the "power play."

SLAP SHOT: Taking a high, hard whack at the puck.

SNIPER: A sharpshooter with a shot at close range.

TIP IN: Deflecting a shot and scoring a goal.

WRAPAROUND: Scoring by slinging the stick around from behind the net.

Suiting Up

Equipment for roller hockey is changing all the time, and there's no end in sight. But the basics remain unchanged: You need to be able to put that biscuit where your team wants it to go.

Roller hockey gear has grown so revolutionary over the past several years that some of its technology has actually been turned around and adapted to the ice game. These days, the sports seem to go back and forth, borrowing new developments from each other. For players who double-dip in both ice and off-ice hockey, there's crossover gear to match.

SKATES

Hockey boots have been around a lot longer than inlines, and roller hockey boots show it. They still use stitched boots, either traditional leather or synthetic ones. Boot stiffness is important for better power transfer, less fatigue, and ankle support in the stress of constant turning and sprinting. Heavier skaters need more boot support. Aim for a super-snug fit, about 1 to 1.5 sizes smaller than your shoe size. As for wheels, there's a trend toward using frames with split setups (as shown), combining larger and smaller wheels to allow for faster acceleration and tighter turns.

STICKS

A good stick is one that best transfers your arm, leg, and rotational movement to the puck. The long part of the stick is called the shaft, while the bottom part that touches the floor is the heel. When held straight up, a properly sized stick will end just below your chin. Topnotch shafts are often aluminum and composite shafts because they tend to be lighter than conventional wood shafts and they're more consistent in feel and perform-ance. Wood gives you a different feel with every stick, and each wood type offers its own distinct properties.

PROTECTIVE GEAR

Start with a hockey helmet and gloves. The more you play, the more gear you should amass. Anyone playing in a fairly serious league will have the full complement: knee and shin guards, elbow pads, shoulder pads, mouthguard, hip protector, pelvic cup, and maybe even a throat protector.

PUCKS VS. BALLS

Balls are typically used on rougher surfaces like asphalt because they roll more smoothly. Some companies even make different balls for varying temperatures: harder for hot weather, softer for cold. Pucks are ideal for smoother surfaces and allow greater control. Roller hockey floors aren't as friction-free as ice, so roller pucks come with plastic runners to help them slide more easily across the floor.

Roll Playing

Put heads together with your teammates and work out some winning strategies for scoring and fending off the enemy.

Gear is great, but it's only as good as your game. Here's what you need to know if you want to become an off-ice all-star.

STICK HANDLING

You've got to keep the ball or puck under control. Start with a proper grip: gloves six inches apart, with each hand's thumb and forefinger creating a downward V, aligned above each other. The next trick is to keep your upper body loose and able to move in any direction. Skating with wide legs will also keep the opposition pondering your next move.

PASSING

The key to a smooth pass is to keep your head up, eyes forward, and push (not slap) the ball or puck with the heel of the stick. Don't lower your bottom hand to pass, or you'll slow yourself down and telegraph your intentions. To receive a pass, keep the stick loose so the biscuit doesn't bounce away.

SHOOTING

Work on speed and accuracy and on making lightning-fast goals from up close. Practice shooting at the different corners of the goal with as little setup time as possible. Get the knack of lifting the puck or ball into the high corners of the net. Follow through on your shots and roll your wrists for a powerful snap.

TEAM TACTICS

Strategy is crucial for organized play. The most common scoring tactic is the triangle offense: Move play to one side of the rink to bring the goalie out of position and open up a scoring opportunity. Power plays are also key opportunities that a good team learns to maximize.

HOCKEY GURUS

U.S.A. Hockey Inline is an offshoot of the governing body of hockey, which is in charge of the U.S. Olympic ice hockey team. U.S.A. Hockey Inline offers a wealth of programs and sanctions leagues around the country. The organization puts together player development clinics and holds tournaments nationwide. Another key resource is U.S.A. Roller Hockey, which does much the same via the organizing body of roller skating. If you're looking for a leg up in the sport, these are two groups you want to get involved with.

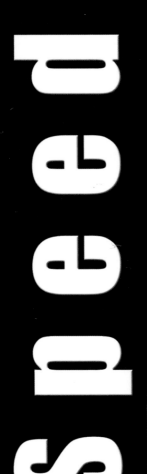

Speed

It's amazing what one extra wheel can do. It's the difference between traveling at mortal speeds and going supersonic. That one little wheel is the all-areas pass for getting into speed and competitive inline racing. Here, the wind wails, your bearings scream, and life passes in a blur.

Take It to the Limit

Get ready to take off into a new dimension of skating. The moves are different, the skates are something else. Do you feel the need for speed?

Speed skating is more than simply skating fast. First, you've got to get the right wheels. You'll also need to learn a new set of strokes and movements, both to build speed and to maintain it so your body doesn't tire out too quickly.

TAKE FIVE

A speed skate has five wheels. A longer wheel platform lets you sit back farther for a faster stride and gives you a bigger surface for pushing out. Speed boots, made of extra lightweight materials, are cut low at the cuff to allow for greater freedom of movement. High-end race boots come with heat-moldable materials and top quality leather. These hard boots will transfer every bit of your energy into the ground. They sit on rigid, super-long frames that are specially designed for extra-large racing wheels.

POWER SKATING

Proper technique for speed means pushing out completely from the heel, practically lifting up your toes. Pros skate with a near 90-degree knee bend, so practice getting lower and lower, even putting your elbows on your knees if you have to. Watch yourself in a mirror to see how low you should be; most people skate higher than they think. As you bring your recovering leg back in, make sure to brush your knees past each other. Then try putting the skate down on its outside wheel edges to lengthen your stroke even more.

DOUBLE TROUBLE

The hottest technique in racing these days is the double-push Chad Hedrick. The skater starts with a wider than usual stance, rolls the pushing skate in underneath the body, and then pushes it back out. The one-two punch of an inside and outside push is now standard procedure with the world's top inline racers.

COURSES OF ACTION

Competitions can be held indoors (also called short track) or out with many different formats.

CRITERIUM: "Crits" are usually timed races held on short courses. Get looped by the lead pack and you're out. To keep the action furious, many races offer mid-race prize incentives called "preems" that go to the racer who crosses the finish line first on a particular lap.

TIME TRIAL: An individual race where skaters battle for the lowest time over a set distance.

TRACK: These competitions are held on an oval track with the top events held on a velodrome, an oval with raised corners.

SPRINTS: Short, fast races ranging from 100 meters to 5 kilometers.

DISTANCE: Short distances are 5 to 10 kilometers. The most common distance is 20 kilometers. Long distance races include 26-mile marathons and can go as long as 100 kilometers.

ULTRA-DISTANCE: These races push the envelope and can last for hours. The most famous event is the 86-mile Athens to Atlanta, which challenges skaters to tackle the rolling countryside hills between these two Georgia cities every October.

STAGE RACE: A single competition combining various races and formats to produce overall winners.

RELAY: A team race, usually indoors, in which the incoming skater pushes the next skater forward for a quick burst of speed.

Spin to Win

There's nothing wrong with just blowing past the recreational skaters in the park, but if you want to take your skills to the competitive edge, you need more than fleet feet.

Racing is more than just skating fast. It takes tactics and specialized maneuvers to improve your time and beat out the competition. Put the following moves into your repertoire, and you'll be off to a quick start.

DRAFTING

Skate behind another skater—a technique called drafting—and you'll either go up to 30 percent faster or keep up the same speed with about 30 percent less effort. That's because you'll save yourself from battling wind resistance. It's no wonder, then, that drafting is the most important aspect of racing aside from fitness.

A group of drafting skaters is called a pack. When drafting downhill with a skater in front, rest the rear of your hand on his or her lower back. This not only keeps you in line with the skater, but also helps boost the pack's speed. Because you're out of the wind, on a downward slope you'll tend to move faster than the person ahead of you does. Do your best to match the stride of the person in front, and take your turn at the front to share the workload.

ARM SWINGS

These can give you an extra burst of power, but use them sparingly because they'll also tire you out. At comfortable paces, rest your clasped hands on your lower back to conserve energy. To speed up, swing your arms gradually back and forth, fully extending at the end of each swing. Make sure your forward swing is in synch with the pushing out of your opposite skate (for example, right hand forward, left leg pushed out). Focus on swinging forward and back, not across. Also, to maintain your balance, make sure not to swing your arm much past the middle of your chest. On corners, only swing the outside arm (the one that faces away from the turn). For sprints, bend your elbows and swing both arms in short bursts.

TACTICAL ADVANTAGE

Learn some key racing tactics.

STARTS: The start is often the fastest and most furious part of a race. Do your best to relax and find a group of skaters who are going at your intended pace. If you're ahead of your intended pack, let them catch up and then speed up slightly as they approach. Be prepared to sprint to latch on as they pass.

FLIERS: To make a break, allow a small gap to form between you and the skater ahead. Then skate forward quickly, get sucked into that person's draft, and use your extra speed to veer to the side and get ahead of the pack. Sprint like mad until you're comfortably ahead, or else duck back into the pack and recharge.

GAPS: If you're trailing the pack, quickly sprint up to close the gap or you'll suddenly find yourself alone. Use the draft to rest if the pace is comfortable for you.

SPEED WOBBLES: If you're literally shaking in your boots at high downhill speeds, stop the wobbles by shifting your weight farther onto your heels. If that doesn't work, lift and lower one skate at a time.

◄ *A pack of skaters*

Down to Extremes

The way to gain some serious speed when you're skating is to go downhill. Let gravity do the work and just let go.

Unlike most inline sports, which had simple beginnings, downhill started at the big time and only later developed a loyal local scene. It began as a made-for-TV event for the original X Games and was canceled a couple of years later. Today its largest following comes from European alpine hotspots like France, Austria, Switzerland, and Italy, where hair-raising mountain switchbacks are in abundance. Here, speed demons push gravity to the max, skating their best not only to win but also to keep themselves in one piece.

TIME TRIALS

Also simply called "inline downhill," these road races run 1.5 kilometers or longer. As in Super G ski races, racers do solo runs and compete for the lowest time. Turns are among the most challenging parts of a course, and racers will sometimes use a sliding turn—getting so far over on their wheel edges that they slide as they carve a corner—and even jump over curbs to speed along unhindered.

BORDERCROSS

This event most closely follows the sport's X Games roots. A race involving groups of skaters, it's done as a series of heats: The fastest skater in each group advances to the next round. More skaters on the course mean more bottlenecks in the corners, and it's as much of a challenge to stay in control as it is to race to the bottom.

MAX SPEED

The course where velocity is king is a very steep hill with no turns. Skaters simply go into a deep tuck and head down. Radar guns measure their speed, though no speeding tickets are issued. These events have been held with the sole aim of setting a new mark in the *Guinness Book of World Records*.

OFF-ROAD

Roces came out with the first dirt-friendly skate some years back, but it was the Rollerblade Coyote that finally put off-road skating on the radar screen. The Coyote features massive air tires with big treads and a disc brake, all with enough height to ride grass slopes. The sport is the most obscure of all the downhill disciplines, but if you want to be a trailblazer, then get the right pair of skates and get off the asphalt.

BREAKING THE BARRIER

There have been tons of claims for top skating speeds—some legitimate, others far-fetched, and still others that are hard to categorize as either fact or fiction. According to the International Inline Downhill Association, the fastest competition record goes to Yvon Labarthe from Switzerland, who at Austria's Zell am See in 1999 peaked at 68 miles per hour. Equally impressive was Jörg Schläfli's assisted speed mark of 190 miles per hour, which the Swiss skater accomplished by being towed behind a motorcycle.

Yvon Labarthe

Extreme
Sports

Part Five

Style

Not into the competitive scene? Maybe you want to use your skates to show off your creative side. Or maybe you just want to have some fun. Get into the rhythm and let your body move to the groove.

Let's Dance

On skates, there's no such thing as two left feet. If you've got the music and the mood, just start rolling. Your feet will do the rest.

Dance is where the skating doesn't start until the DJ gets rolling. Just like regular dancing, the skate version has lots of different styles and allows lots of personal expression.

ARTISTICALLY SPEAKING

Artistic inline figure skating is for those who have a competitive edge; it has a format and style that's just like ice figure skating. Yes, even with the costumes and romantic music. Dance styles judged in competitions include freestyle (with jumps and spins), creative solo (usually freestyle without jumps and spins), team dance, and tango for pairs. All of the action is overseen by U.S.A. Roller Skating, which sanctions competitions all across America. Events use the same formats as the Winter Olympics: pairs, freestyle, and compulsory dance.

ROLLER BOOGIE

If letting loose and having fun is more your style, freestyle is your speed. Indoor rinks generally offer skating to disco or modern pop music. If the outdoors are more your thing, cities like New York and San Francisco have huge outdoor hip-hop and funk dance scenes that have been going for decades, free of charge. The rules are that there are no rules. Just look good, cop moves from the regulars, and keep to the beat.

LINE 'EM UP

Line dancing is not only fun, but you can let someone else decide your next step. You'll learn some interesting combinations and will be amazed at how impressive even simple moves look when a large group of skaters performs them in synch.

STEPPIN' OUT

So you don't skate like you have two left feet, get into the following dance basics.

HEEL-TOE SPIN: Wind your arms and shoulders to one side, and then smoothly throw them into the opposite direction to get yourself spinning. As you do this, pop your braking skate onto its rear wheel and your other skate onto its front wheel. While spinning, pick a single object and make it the only thing you look at as you come around each time. Bringing your hands in toward your chest will make you spin faster.

ONE-FOOT TURN: Practice skating and balancing on one foot at a time. Next, try hopping on one skate, correcting your balance with your hips as you land. Finally, hop up and turn 180 degrees to land backward on the same skate, keeping your non-rolling skate behind you for balance.

RUNNING MAN: The inline variation of Michael Jackson's classic moonwalk. Place one skate on its front wheel and slowly move it backwards. As it goes behind you, lift the other skate up on its toe and do the same thing. Put it all together by slowly moving your arms in a running motion. Your whole body should now be rolling in a slow-mo run.

◀ *Skaters dance in New York City's Central Park.*

Into the Night

There's no better way to beat the heat in summer than skating at night. But it isn't much fun alone—nor is it safe. So get adult permission, get a group together, wait till sundown, and go.

Cities all over the world offer night skating groups, with numbers ranging from tens to the thousands. With routes often changing each week, it's a great way to explore different neighborhoods and make the city your urban playground.

EVENING WEAR

For night skates, add reflective wear to your standard protective gear. The most common accessories are blinking lights that clip onto helmets, arms, hip bags, or anywhere else obvious so passing cars and bicycles will see you. Other items include reflective vests, clothing with reflective strips, and reflective stickers that you can glue onto helmets and skates.

CITY NIGHTS

Night skates can happen just about anywhere. The best scenes are mainly in big cities where there's plenty of pavement and lots to see. Skates usually last a couple of hours, but the social dynamic makes you forget how long you've been out. If you're traveling to another city, get in touch with the local skate club and find out if they have a weekly night skate.

TRAVEL ROUNDUP

Check out some of the best urban night-skating scenes on the planet.

NEW YORK: Manhattan is a skating paradise with pavement that is unbelievably smooth, remarkable in a city famous for its potholes. There are two long-running night groups here. Blade Night Manhattan gets hundreds together for a social skate through the Big Apple. A faster group, Tuesday Night Skaters, averages packs of about 30. They always leave Manhattan to explore the outer boroughs and New Jersey—expect to cross at least one bridge.

PARIS: The French enthusiasm for skating has produced the world's largest and most impressive night skate. More than 12,000 skaters have regularly shown up for these weekly events, to the annoyance of motorists who have to wait half an hour while the never-ending string of skaters rolls by. Luckily, the cops out front make sure the skaters have the right of way.

SAN FRANCISCO: The California Outdoor Roller Association (CORA) organizes one of the world's oldest night skates. The route takes hundreds of skaters up, down, and across the city's streets, including some of the steepest cable car-lined thoroughfares that make San Francisco famous.

HOUSTON: The Texas metropolis is a virtual paradise for night skaters, offering events just about every night of the week. The local Skate Trash club offers some wildly themed skates, each one crazier than the last. If you see a bunch of sunglass-wearing skaters with bushy sideburns and flashy jumpsuits, you've probably witnessed the Elvis skate. How about mandatory tuxes and dresses for the Prom skate?

Cone Heads

If you're constantly on edge—wheel edges, that is—you're probably a slalom fan. And if you can't hit the ski slopes, get your skates and line up some plastic cones. Now you're ready to roll.

Slalom is one skating activity that can be done just about anywhere: All it takes is a handful of cones and a smooth strip of pavement. Go forward, backward, sideways, and just about anywhere in between. The faster and smoother you move, the better.

SET 'EM UP

Putting together a proper slalom course is a snap. Those in the know use small cones with their square bases cut off so they don't trip skaters. But you can use anything from plastic bottles or used wheels to cups. A typical course spaces the cones six feet apart on a gradual downhill, although the cones can be as close as two to three feet to increase the technical challenge.

INS AND OUTS

The first technique to master is the forward slalom. Keep your knees bent and skates together and maneuver around each cone like a skier. Hold your upper body still and let your legs and hips do all the work. Shift your weight to change direction quickly, and squat down onto your edges to turn. Next up is the criss-cross, where you cross one skate in front of the other and roll over the cone with your legs in an X. Many skaters remove their heel brakes for this maneuver. You can also test your balance with a one-foot slalom, using your hips to move you from edge to edge. Sounds easy? Now try each move going backward.

LEARNING CURVE

The top-of-the-line slalom tricks make you go sideways or require complicated foot action. Sidesurfing, or gliding sideways around cones, is a great start. This can be upgraded to an independent, in which your sidesurfing feet take turns crisscrossing over each cone. Once you've mastered several moves, put together a combination in a single run. Combine an independent with a forward and backward crisscross, and you've got a run called a shopping cart.

Skating the cones heel-to-heel ▶

SMOOTH MOVES

MONOLINE: One skate follows in the direct path behind the other.

RATTLESNAKE: A backward monoline.

SNAKING: Jumping into the slalom course when it's not your turn (a no-no).

TANDEM: Carving the cones with the rear skate raised onto its front wheel.

ALTERNATING: Switching around the leading and following skates.

EXTENDED: One skate riding on its rear wheel.

TRANSITION: Changing between moves. The result is a combination run.

CUTBACK: Lifting up and crossing one skate behind the other so that your legs are alternately crossed over every cone.

Four-by-Fours

Take the four wheels of your skate and arrange them in two pairs of two. What do you get? None other than the quad, the original roller skate. Not only are quads back in, they're downright fashionable again.

It wasn't long ago that quads, otherwise known as conventional roller skates, were deemed the uncool, outdated cousins of inline skates. Oh, how times have changed. Quads are making a strong comeback, their appeal coming from their retro '70s and '80s look.

QUADS VS. INLINES

There's been a lot of heated debate over which type of skate is better, and the answer is: neither. Quads and inlines are just different, each with its own advantages and drawbacks. Compared to inlines, conventional skates are more stable to stand on and turn on a dime. The extra maneuverability comes from a shorter wheelbase and a plate that tilts the wheels when you lean. The other obvious difference is the brake, a rubber stopper in front that is more intuitive to use and well suited to the flat wooden floors of roller rinks. As for striding, you still push out, but the balance point and feel are slightly different.

ROLLER SPORTS

Quads continue to be used for various skating segments. They have a particularly important role with ball hockey, an internationally-played competitive version of roller hockey similar to field hockey that uses a rounded cane stick and a rubber ball usually on a cement surface. Ball hockey using quads is especially big in Canada, primarily during the summer when the ice has been removed from arenas. Plus, in old-school, NHL-style roller hockey leagues that allow checking, certain players don quads for the extra stability to withstand a direct hit.

Artistic skaters have always used conventional skates in large numbers thanks to tighter turning and extra balance for difficult maneuvers. On the other hand, racing is all about top speeds, so while quad competitions still exist, inlines have proven their superiority. The rarest roller breed is the vert quad skater, and it's fascinating to watch a skater in quads sidesurfing up the half-pipe walls.

RINK REQUIREMENTS

Most people experience quad skating at their local indoor rink, with throngs of skaters spinning under clubby lights to a pulsing beat. While there are various types of quad skates, the standard is a figure-style skate. This usually means a leather or (less preferable and cheaper) vinyl boot, balancing foot support with flexibility to move. How comfortable the skate is depends on a snug but pain-free fit and a well broken-in boot. Beneath the boot is the metal plate (also called the truck), which permits the angled tilt that gets the wheels to turn. As with inlines, the wider quad wheels come in various sizes and hardness and ride on precision-rated bearings.

Safe and Sound

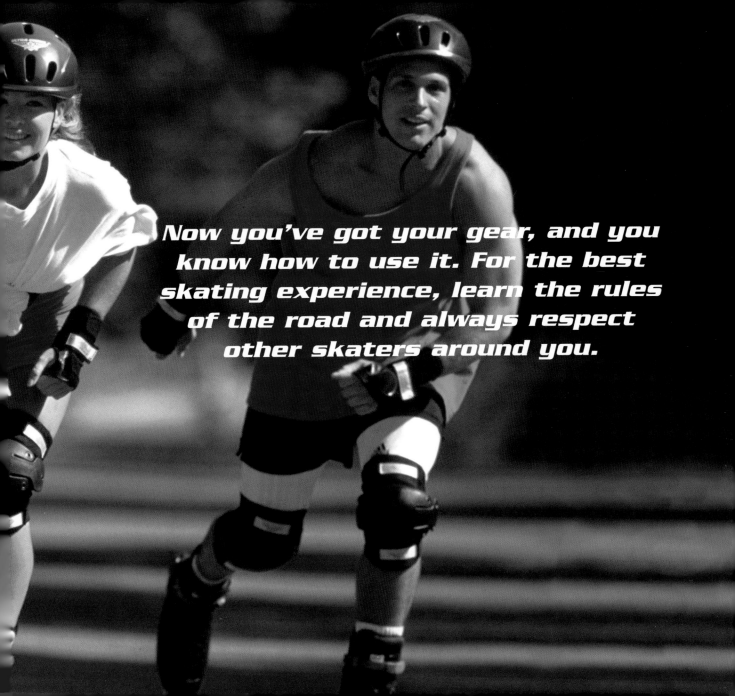

Now you've got your gear, and you know how to use it. For the best skating experience, learn the rules of the road and always respect other skaters around you.

Skate Smart

Skating lessons are a good idea for any beginner. The sport is easy to learn, and the more moves you know how to do, the more fun it is. Taking lessons is also the best way to avoid injuries.

You've certainly run into that person before. You know, the one who says that skating is dangerous, points out those people who crash in the park, and won't do anything more thrilling than shuffleboard. But the truth is that skating is a safe sport, as long as you know your limitations and are smart enough to skate safely.

SAFETY LESSONS

Studies show that half of the people who injure themselves skating have never taken a lesson, while only 11 percent of injuries go to those who've taken 6 or more lessons. So the first thing to do is learn how to skate. It's just as important as protective gear. Not convinced? Consider that only 7 percent of people wearing protective gear have injuries. The most common injuries are at the wrist. These are easily prevented by wearing the right gear.

NATIONAL SKATE PATROL

The NSP is a volunteer program whose members patrol parks, trails, and roads with the aim of keeping skaters safe and ensuring a positive coexistence with cyclists, runners, and pedestrians. The red-shirted patrollers offer a variety of free services, including stopping clinics, first-aid assistance, and tips to skaters on safety and proper etiquette. The patrols allow people to give back to the sport and promote skating as a positive influence in the community. Ask any skate patroller which types get injured the most, and you'll hear similar stories. The boyfriend who's never skated went out the first time without protective gear, showed off for his girlfriend, and took a nasty spill; the woman who went flying downhill on skates, without taking a braking lesson; or the guy wearing the heavy backpack who fell backward without a helmet. What it all comes down to is using your head, plain and simple.

ROAD RULES

When you're out and about on your skates, make sure to follow the IISA's Rules of the Road to keep yourself and those around you happy. These guidelines are easy to remember as *SLAP: Smart, Legal, Alert, and Polite*. Check it out.

SMART

- Always wear protective gear.
- Master the basics: striding, stopping and turning.
- Keep your equipment in working order.

LEGAL

- Obey all traffic regulations.
- Observe the same obligations as a bicyclist or car driver.

ALERT

- Skate under control at all times.
- Watch out for road hazards and avoid water, oil, and sand.
- Avoid heavy traffic.

POLITE

- Skate on the right, pass on the left.
- Announce your intentions by saying, "Passing on your left."
- Always yield to pedestrians.
- Be a goodwill ambassador for the sport.

Maintaining Your Gear

Learn the ABCs of taking care of your gear. It's not as hard or messy as you'd think, and it'll extend the life of your skates. So get out your tools!

Regular maintenance is the key to keeping you and your skates happy, and while you can pay a skate shop to do it, you'll save a lot by doing it yourself. Although it can seem intimidating at first, maintenance is easy with practice. The more you do it on your own, the more likely you'll keep it up regularly. Besides, you never know when you'll need to fix a problem on the roll.

BEARINGS

Bearings are the part of your skate most susceptible to the elements, and they'll slow you down if left to collect dirt or rust. They're also expensive, but you can extend the life of your bearings with occasional upkeep. How often you clean them depends on how often you skate. Consider doing at least two cleanings each season.

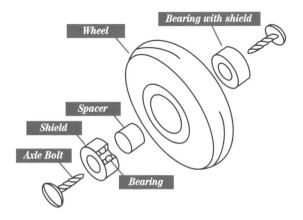

To clean, you'll need a rag or two, plus a solvent (such as a citrus degreaser), bearing lube, a small screwdriver, and a punch tool that you can buy at any skate shop. Unscrew all the skate's axle bolts, and take out the wheels. Next, insert the punch tool in the center of each wheel and push hard. The two bearings and their spacers should pop right out. Each bearing is covered by a shield. Remove these with the small screwdriver. Then put the bearings, shields, bolts, spacers, and axle bolts in a jar filled with the solvent. Drain the solvent after a few minutes.

Spin the bearings a few times to clear them out, and then place everything on a clean rag to dry for an hour or so. Finally, put a drop or two of lube into each bearing, put all the parts back together, and you're off!

WHEELS

The sad fact is, your wheels will wear down, and they'll wear unevenly. The more of a beginner you are, the more likely you will grind down your front wheels and batter your outside edges, giving your wheels a lopsided profile. This is especially noticeable if you T-stop or powerslide. To minimize this effect and extend the life of your wheels, rotate them regularly. Remove all four wheels and switch the largest with the smallest and the second-largest with the second-smallest. It's also a good idea to swap the wheels to the opposite skate, placing them so the worn outside edges are on the inside. All this will even your wheels out over time. And don't forget to replace worn brakes before they grind down too far, unless you enjoy drilling out ruined bolt-screws.

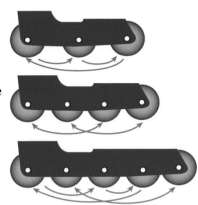

Wheel rotation placement ▲

Work It

It's easy to get better at skating, and you don't even need to join a gym or exercise class. Just get out there!

S kating is good exercise. And unlike running, it won't do a number on your knees and ankles. Here's what you need to know if you want to train to be a stronger, better skater.

TRAINING WHEELS

If you want to build strength and endurance, go for long skates at a moderate pace, increasing your skating time by about ten percent each week. Make a plan to go skating between three to five days a week. Start your workout by skating continuously for at least 20 minutes. It's a good idea to undertake a fitness plan with a buddy—you don't have to do your workout all alone, and you and your friend can motivate each other to reach your goals.

THE LONG HAUL

To increase endurance, skate at easy to medium intensities. You'll benefit most from an extra long skate once a week. Start out at a pace that feels almost too easy. This will allow you to skate continuously for a long period and get your body used to working overtime. To keep your body fueled, keep nibbling at an energy bar, especially if you're skating past the one-hour mark.

SET YOUR SIGHTS

Power and speed are the hardest to achieve and the easiest to lose. You reach them only through short but intense workout sessions. A simple technique is *fartlek*, a Swedish term meaning "speed play." It works by picking a distant object such as a tree or street sign and racing to it. Once you've reached your target, slow down to rest until you're ready to pick another object. Try varying the intervals between skating hard and resting, but remember that the higher the intensity, the shorter the workout should be.

FITNESS GEAR

Skating longer and faster for fitness means that you'll want a particularly comfortable, breathable, and high-performance skate. This typically features a softer boot, top-notch wheels and bearings, and longer frames. Together, they'll help you go the distance without wasting unnecessary energy. Clothing should be comfortable and made of breathable materials. For protective gear, many fitness skaters prefer a good bike helmet that's air-cooled plus a slim wrist guard. A water bottle holder or hydration pack is crucial.

To Find Out More...

ORGANIZATIONS

International Inline Skating
Association (IISA)
201 North Front Street,
Suite 306
Wilmington, NC 28401
(910) 762-7004
www.iisa.org

U.S.A. Hockey InLine
1775 Bob Johnson Drive
Colorado Springs, CO
80906-4090
(719) 576-8724
www.usahockey.org

U.S.A. Roller Sports
(The national governing body
of inline and roller skating)
4730 South St., P.O. Box 6579
Lincoln, NE 68506-1465
(402) 483-7551
www.usarollersports.com

Aggressive Skaters Association
(The organizer of the
popular ASA Pro Tour)
13468 Beach Ave.
Marina Del Ray, CA 90292
(310) 823-1865
www.asaskate.com

WEB SITES

Skating the Infobahn
www.skatecity.com/Index/

About.com Inline Pages
http://inlineskating.about.com

Skating.com
www.skating.com

Be-Mag
www.be-mag.com

Aggressive.com
www.aggressive.com

Daily Bread
www.dbmag.com

Speedskating.com
www.speedskating.com

*Fitness and
Speedskating Times*
www.fasst.com

InlineDownhill.com
www.inlinedownhill.com

Inline Hockey Central
www.inlinehockeycentral.com

ABOUT THE AUTHOR

Michael Shafran has written about everything inline imaginable. Past positions include editor and founder of Skating.com, editor of *InLine Retailer & Industry News*, inline editor for *MetroSports Magazine*, and skate market analyst for Sporting Goods Business. He's also a regular contributor to *InLine* magazine and *Men's Journal*. A longtime competitive inline racer and night skater, Michael has been a Central Park Skate Patroller, a certified IISA instructor, and a co-founder of New York's Empire Speed club. Nowadays, he serves as the Chief Sub-Editor for *Ralph*, Australia's largest men's magazine, and he regularly night skates with the Sydney Bladers.

PHOTO CREDITS

Cover: PhotoDisc; Chris Covatta/Getty Images: Pages 2–3, 42, 63; Adam Pretty/Getty Images/ESPN: Pages 4–5; Mike Powell /Getty Images: Page 6; K2 Sports: Pages 7, 13, 19; Rollerblade™: Pages 8–9, 12, 43, 51; Corbis: Pages 10, 15; John Greenstreet: Pages 14, 25, 50, 53, 58, 59; Al Bello/Getty Images: Page 16; Bauer Nike Hockey, Inc.: Pages 17, (stick, skate, gloves, helmet) 35, 55; Image Source: Page 18; Hemera/Ablestock: Pages 20–21; Stanley Chou/Getty Images: Pages 22, 28; PhotoDisc: Pages 23, 26, 27, 32, (ball) 35, 38–39; Kenneth Greer/courtesy of Steve Kay: Page 24; John Ferry/Getty Images: Page 29; Phil Cole/Getty Images: Pages 30–31, 34, 54; J.D. Cuban/Getty Images: Pages 33, 36; Propuck Inc.: (puck) Page 35; USA Hockey: Page 37; Séverine Arcioni: Pages 40, 45; Bont International: Page 41; Donald Miralle/Getty Images: Page 44; Bob Nichols: Pages 45–46, 55; Steve Kay: Pages 48, 49; Ryan Shawgo/courtesy of Jeffrey DeCola: Page 52; Al Bello/Getty Images: Pages 55–56; Bob "Bobarazzi" Ryan: Page 60; Tim DeFrisco/Getty Images: Page 62

Library of Congress Cataloging-in-Publication Data
Shafran, Michael.
Skate!: your guide to inline, aggressive, vert, street, roller hockey, speed skating, dance, fitness training, and more /by Michael Shafran.
p. cm. — (Extreme sports)
Summary: Provides instruction in everything from standing on skates for the first time to dancing or excercising on them.
ISBN 0-7922-5107-5 (pbk.)
1. In-line skating—Juvenile literature.
2. Extreme sports—Juvenile literature. [1. In-line skating.
2. Roller skating. 3. Extreme sports.] I. Title.
II. Series: Extreme sports (Washington, D.C.)
GV859.73.S53 2003 796.21–dc21 2002012765

Design: Todd Cooper, Sonia Gauba, designlabnyc
Editorial: J. A. Ball Associates
Series Design: Joy Masoff